For Debbie & Sean,

Thank you very much!

My South Coast Home

PHOTOGRAPHS OF THE MISSISSIPPI GULF COAST

Ken Murphy

Ken Murphy

SOUTH COAST PUBLISHING   BAY ST. LOUIS

DEDICATED TO

TINA, DYLAN, NICOLETTE,

AND CHRISTINA

MY BEAUTIFUL FAMILY

Copyright © 2001 Ken Murphy
2ND Edition Copyright © 2006
ISBN 0-9788450-0-5
ISBN 978-0-9788450-0-1

Printed in China by Everbest Printing
Designed and produced by John A. Langston

Ken Murphy
221 Leonhard Avenue
Bay St. Louis, MS 39520
228-467-5999
kenmurphysouth@aol.com
kenmurphysouth.com

PRECEDING PAGES:
North Beach Blvd., Bay St. Louis
Iris, Lakeshore
Cedar Point, Bay St. Louis
South Beach Blvd, Bay St. Louis

RIGHT: Pine tree and Cherokee Rose, Log Town

Preface

I believe that some things are just meant to be—let's call it Fate. This, my first book, is one of them.

The chain of events that led me to photography began with an accident that occurred while I was serving in the U.S. Army as a Tank Commander. It was 1975, and I had just been transferred to Mannheim, Germany, from Fort Knox, Kentucky. Before we left for Germany, however, we went through the U.S. Army Armor School.

While there, the Army checks everyone's records. I was told that I needed a secondary Military Occupational Specialty (MOS), just in case something happened to me. The records clerk asked me what I wanted it to be. I laughed! The Army was actually asking me what I wanted it to be? Half jokingly, I said, "Hell, I don't know what I want to be when I grow up!" The clerk replied, "You have to have one, so pick something, and hurry up!" In steps Fate. "Give me something in Special Services," I said. He typed something on paper (a time before computers) and put it in my records. I didn't give it a second thought, until some months later when I got a set of orders telling me that my secondary MOS was 03 Delta, an Arts & Crafts Specialist. It was a big joke around the motor pool. It seemed ridiculous to go from training

people to kill one day, to training them in a hobby the next. I never thought I would use it. That's what I get for thinking!

The next event, a somewhat traumatic one (I've never had a nightmare about the accident), brought me one step closer to my destiny (or the publication of *My South Coast Home*). I had been in the field for fourteen days, and it was the last day, the last ten minutes of the exercise, and we were on our way to the rail head to put our tanks on the train for the ride home. We were waiting in the wood line of a field, planning to attack a unit on the other side. Some of the tanks had a new toy, a Hoffman Device, which simulates the main gun firing during maneuvers. I didn't have one, nor did I want one (just something else to clean). Anyway, I was ordered to take the Hoffman Device off of a tank that had just broken down. After arguing with my superior for a few minutes, rank won, which means I lost. To make a much longer story just long, the numbers 1 and 2 tubes discharged prematurely. My right hand was in the way. The result—my right index finger was gone, and I had major damage to my thumb and middle finger.

Once again, the Army asked me what I wanted to do and where I wanted to be stationed. Once again, I laughed. (Now they were going to send me to any station I wanted. Right!)

Well, I said anywhere in California, Washington State, or Alaska, so of course they sent me to Fort Leonhard Wood, Missouri (three thousand miles from where I wanted to be), where I would be working in the wood crafts area of the Special Services, Arts and Crafts Facility, with saws and other dangerous power tools! Amazing! I was actually using my secondary MOS and I was in danger of losing more fingers. Is that irony or what?

This was a brand new, million dollar recreational facility, with all sorts of arts and crafts, including photography. Once again, Fate intervened. Not long after my arrival, the guy running the photo section got fired. Since I was the lowest member on the totem pole, I was chosen to take over the photography section, temporarily, while they searched for a replacement. Forget the fact that I didn't even know how to load a 35mm camera. Fate, in the form of a little old lady (I wish I could remember her name), taught me the basics of black and white developing and printing. "This is cool stuff!" I thought. I soon fell in love with photography, and after several months of teaching myself how to take photographs, I entered one of my shots (The Corn Shed), in an Army Worldwide Photo Contest. Much to my surprise and delight, I won third place in the color landscape division, receiving a certificate and a $75 Savings Bond. I was hooked!

For the first time in my life, I had something that I truly loved to do, and it even felt like me! I asked if I could keep the photography instructor position, and my boss, Fred Early, said yes! I was in heaven for three years! (They even tried to promote me but I wouldn't take it for fear of losing my position in the photo section.) The Army provided me with everything I needed—equipment, film paper, chemistry, you name it. It was the best job I ever had. From then on, when someone would ask me about my finger, I would tell them that I traded it for a camera.

After leaving the Army, I listened to the voices saying, "Go West, crazy man, go West!" and headed to Tempe, Arizona, with the intent of entering the photography program at Arizona State University. (I arrived in town with $500, no job, and no place to live.) Unfortunately, I couldn't afford it, even with my G.I. benefits. After about six months, the "concrete desert" got the best of me, so I loaded up my Carmengia, put my other belongings on a train, and headed to Tacoma, Washington, to stay with my younger brother Tim. While in Tacoma, I worked in The Camera Shop, selling photography stuff and dreaming of becoming a professional photographer. That lasted almost a year, but I soon got homesick and moved back to Bay St. Louis, where I convinced my mom Helen Dedeaux Murphy Decell, to hock the house, and she, Tim, and I founded Dan B's (named after my deceased dad, Dan Beverly Murphy), a small neighborhood bar on the beach in downtown Bay St. Louis. That same year I married my beautiful wife Tina. After almost three years, I burned out, which is when Fate sent Louis Decell to marry my mother and take over the business. After twenty-one years, they are still there.

The timing was perfect! I decided that there must be a better way to make a living; I could go to college on a VA, Disabled Veterans Vocational Rehabilitation program. I discovered the Rochester Institute of Technology (RIT) in Rochester, New York, one of the world's best colleges for studying photography, and enrolled into the photography program where I pursued a BFA in Narrative, Documentary, and Editorial Photography. The rest as they say, is history.

After graduating, I came back to the South Coast for about six months, but I couldn't find any work, so we packed up and moved to New Orleans, where I worked as an assistant for several photographers. After about three years (there must be something about three years) we couldn't take the big city life any longer and moved back home, to my small portion of the South Coast. (The South Coast encompasses Florida, Alabama, Mississippi, Texas, and Mexico, if you want to get technical.) I got a job with the original *Coast Magazine*, where I honed my shooting skills. I also started shooting for the Hancock Bank Calendar, which provided me opportunities to build my photo file. Many of those photos are in this book.

My South Coast Home is an eclectic book of photographs that I have made over the last twelve or so years, either on assignment or just for the fun of it, primarily in the Bay St. Louis and Hancock County areas. They are not intended as a historic record or an all inclusive exposé. Also, many of the photographs have no dates given. Many of the scenes have changed or are gone all together. I hope, though, when viewed as a group, the photographs capture the essence of this place—the people, the water, Biloxi Bacon (mullet), the fishing and floundering (My daughter Christina and I got four last night), the laid back way of life, the smell of fresh, hot French bread from the Bobby Ann Bakery on Main St., the bayous, the gators, the Islands, the thick forests of evergreen trees, the smell of the heavy, humid, salt air on a still summer sunrise, the crawfish, shrimp, and crab boils. The list can go on. However, photographs alone cannot capture the entire experience.

It is this essence of *My South Coast Home*, along with my family and my memories of an idyllic childhood (although money was very hard to come by), that have brought me home.

Those who know me will attest to the fact that I could go on and on. However, I will be merciful and sum things up. Basically I took a look at the collection of photographs that I have of this area and decided to hock the family land, begin a publishing company, and publish a coffee table book. That should be easy enough! My family thinks I'm a little too far out over the water. At any rate, I hope you enjoy this selection of photographs as much as I have enjoyed making them.

From the Publisher

I first met Ken Murphy several years ago when he was taking my photograph for a cover of *Coast Magazine.* I have followed his work through the years and I've been repeatedly impressed.

Like me, I think you will find that Ken has a special eye for capturing a unique perspective on film—regardless of his subject. What makes this book so appealing is the fact that the book melds Ken's passion for photography with his undying love of the Mississippi Gulf Coast.

Frankly, what you are holding in your hands is a collective snapshot of our community, a compilation that was twelve years in the making.

In a previous book, *Biloxi: 300 Years,* we used photographs and words to tell the colorful and exciting story of our historic community. In this latest effort, we try to capture some of the essence of this place we call home. Leafing through these pages, we hope you will discover some of the things that make our home the special place that it is.

I believe that it is important that we have books like *Biloxi: 300 Years* and *My South Coast Home.* They provide a timeless document that shows our changing way of life, how we've grown, and just as importantly, how we have stayed the same.

It was Thomas Wolfe who wrote a book called *You Can't Go Home Again.* Looking through these pages, seeing our community through the eyes of Ken Murphy, you will wonder why some people would ever want to leave home.

I thank my family as well as David Washer of Coast Community Bank and Vincent Creel of the City of Biloxi for their help and support on this project.

Finally, I hope that you find as much enjoyment looking at this book as I have found in bringing it to you.

Edward Gemmill

St. Stanislaus Pier, Bay St. Louis

Pass Christian Small Craft Harbor

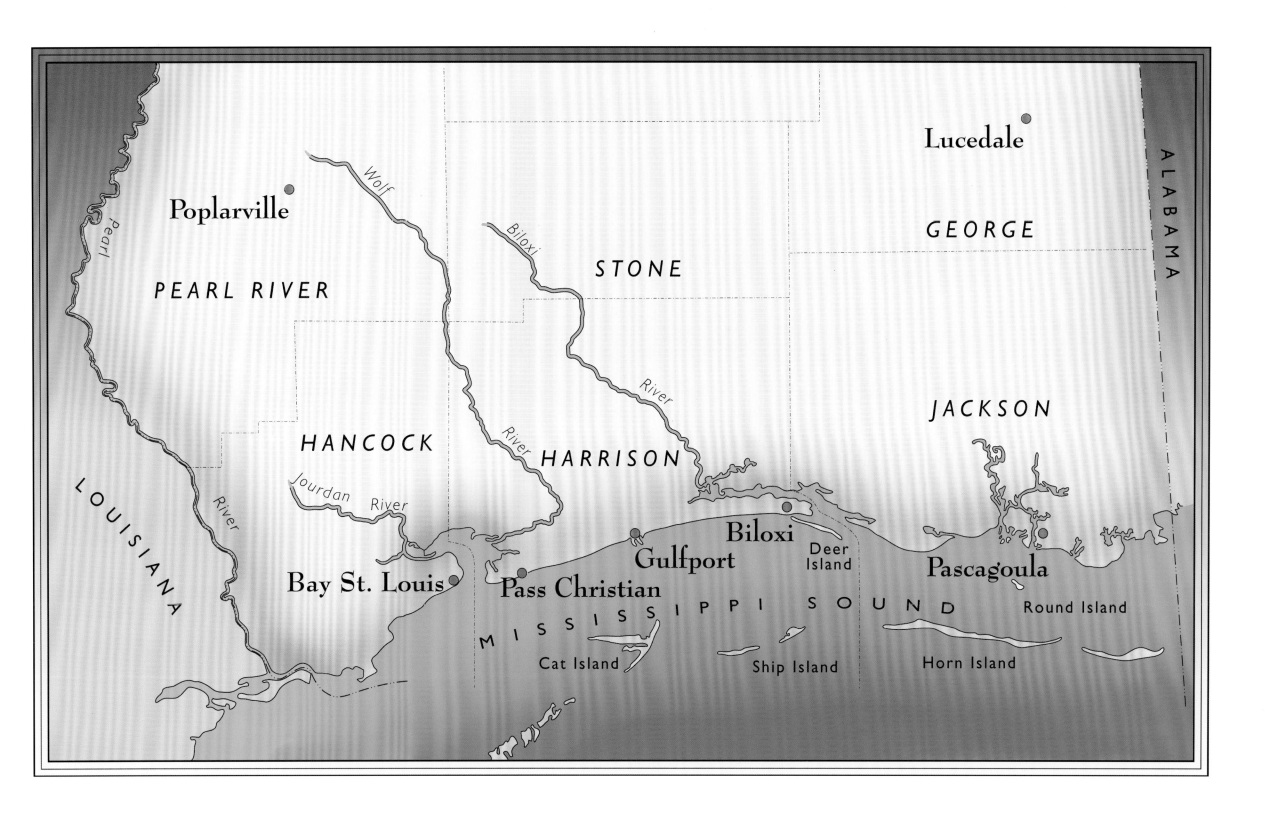

South Beach Blvd., Bay St. Louis

My South Coast Home

PLATE I: *South Beach Blvd., Bay St. Louis*

3

PLATE 2: *Point Clear Island, Hancock County*

PLATES 3 AND 4: *Joe's Bayou, Bay St. Louis*

7

PLATE 5: *Marsh, Hancock County*

9

PLATES 6 AND 7: *Bordage's Fish Camp, Lakeshore; (above) Wolf and Ray Bordage*

11

PLATE 8: *Spotted "Speck" Sea Trout*

12

PLATE 9: *Bird track, South Beach Blvd., Bay St. Louis*
PLATE 10: *Blue Claw Crab, Bay St. Louis*

13

PLATE 11: *Back Bay, Biloxi*

15

PLATE 12: *North Beach Blvd., Bay St. Louis*

16

PLATE 13: *Brown Pelican, Waveland*

17

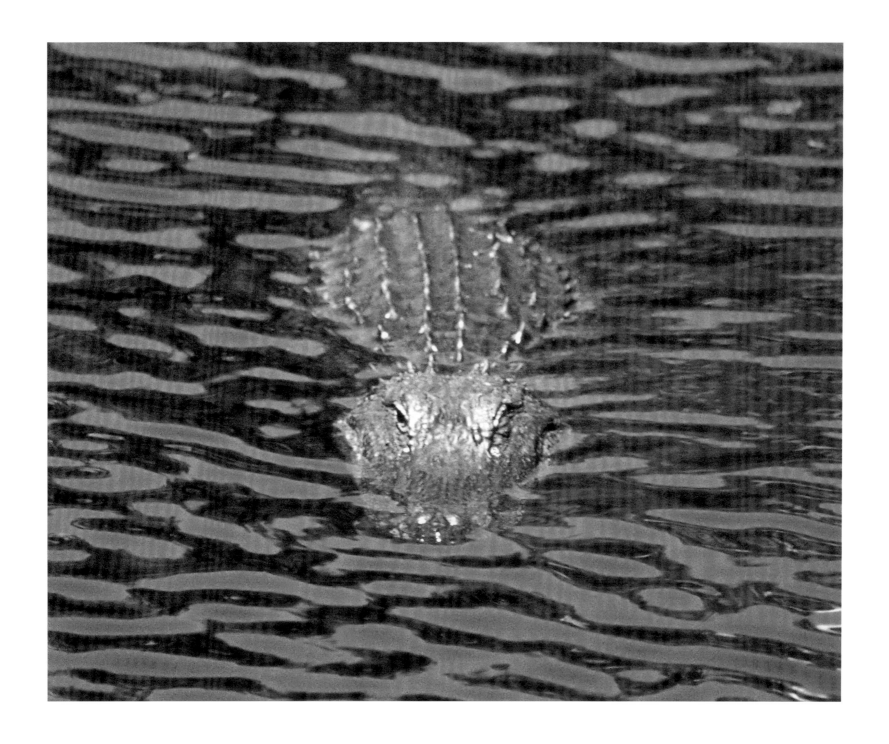

PLATE 14: *Alligator*

19

PLATE 15: *Gulls on Ship Island*

PLATE 16: *South Beach Blvd., Bay St. Louis*

23

PLATE 17: *Pier, Waveland*

25

PLATE 18: *Cowan Bayou, Pearlington*

27

PLATE 19: *Monroe's Pier, Waveland*

PLATE 20: *Cedar Point, Bay St. Louis*

PLATE 22: *Cedar Point, Bay St. Louis*

33

PLATE 23: *Cruisin' the Coast, 1999, downtown, Bay St. Louis*

34

PLATE 24: *Cruisin' the Coast, 2000, Pass Christian*
PLATE 25: *Cruisin' the Coast, 1997, Main Street, Bay St. Louis*

PLATE 26: *Gator Rescue, Beach Blvd., Waveland*

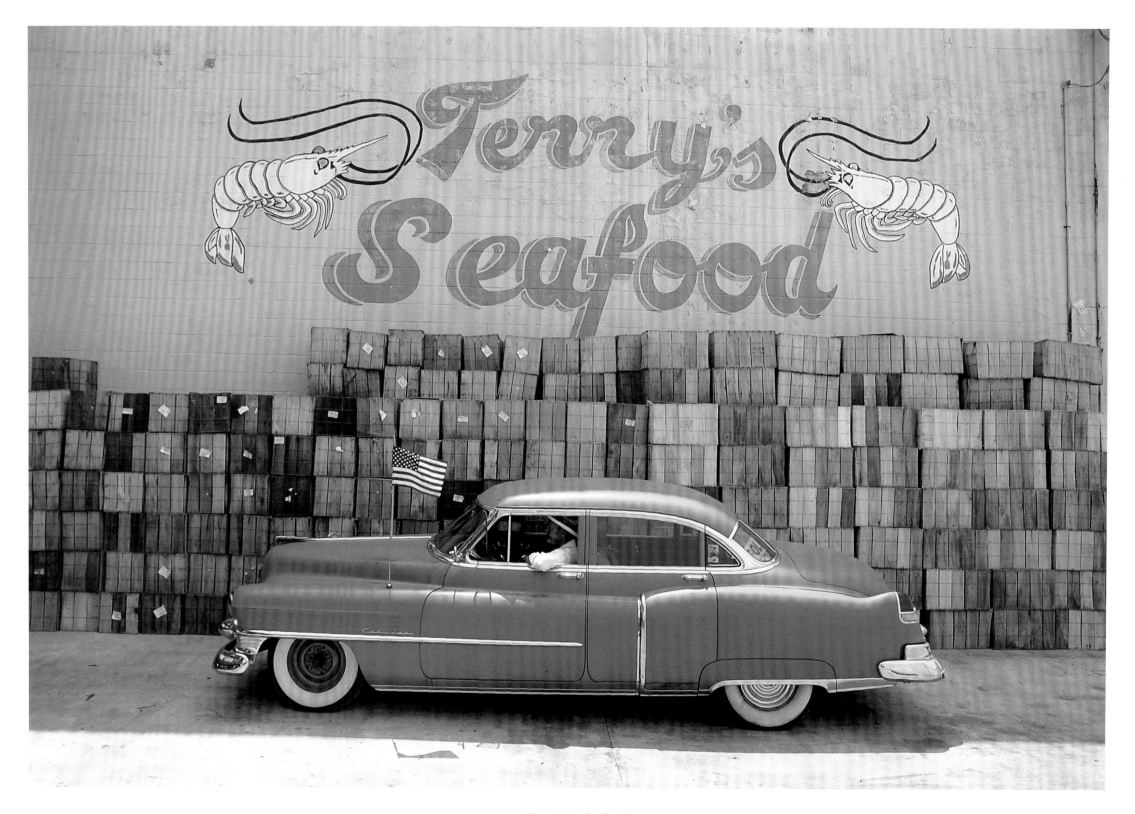

PLATE 27: *Terry's Seafood, Lakeshore*

37

PLATE 28: *Al Kingston, Barber, Bay St. Louis*

PLATE 29: *Church, Pearlington*

40

PLATE 30: *United Methodist Gulfside Assembly, Waveland*

PLATE 31: *Chicken on Fence, Hancock Street, Bay St. Louis*

42

PLATE 32: *St. Charles Street, Bay St. Louis*

43

PLATE 33: *North Beach Blvd., Bay St. Louis*

45

PLATE 34: *St. Rose de Lima Catholic Church, Bay St. Louis*

46

PLATE 35: *Mural, St. Rose de Lima Catholic Church, Bay St. Louis*

47

PLATE 36: *Annunciation Catholic Church, Kiln*

PLATE 37: *Pier at Easter, Waveland*

50

PLATE 38: *Koch Grave, Log Town*

52

PLATE 39: *Wheat Grave, near Poplarville*

PLATE 40: *Crosby Arboretum, Picayune*

55

PLATE 41: *Tung tree, Gum Pond, Pearl River County*

PLATE 42: *Pearl River, Log Town Launch, Log Town*

PLATE 43: *Shrimp boat at sunrise, Mississippi Sound*

61

PLATE 44: *Pitcher plant bog, Log Town*
PLATE 45: *Forest floor, Log Town*

62

PLATE 46: *Oak tree, Log Town*

63

PLATE 47: *The Wall, Waveland*

64

PLATE 48: *The Door, Waveland*

PLATE 50: *Lizard on banana leaf, Bay St. Louis*
PLATE 51: *Gopher Tortoise, Red Creek Wildlife Management Area, Stone County*

68

PLATE 52: *Hawk in oak tree, Bay St. Louis*

69

PLATE 53: *Magnolia, Bay St. Louis*

70

PLATE 54: *Mark Murphy with Champion Magnolia, Leaf River Wildlife Management Area, Perry County*

PLATE 55: *Pascagoula River, near Benndale, George County*

PLATE 56: *West end, Cat Island*

PLATE 57: *Oak tree and moss, Cat Island*

76

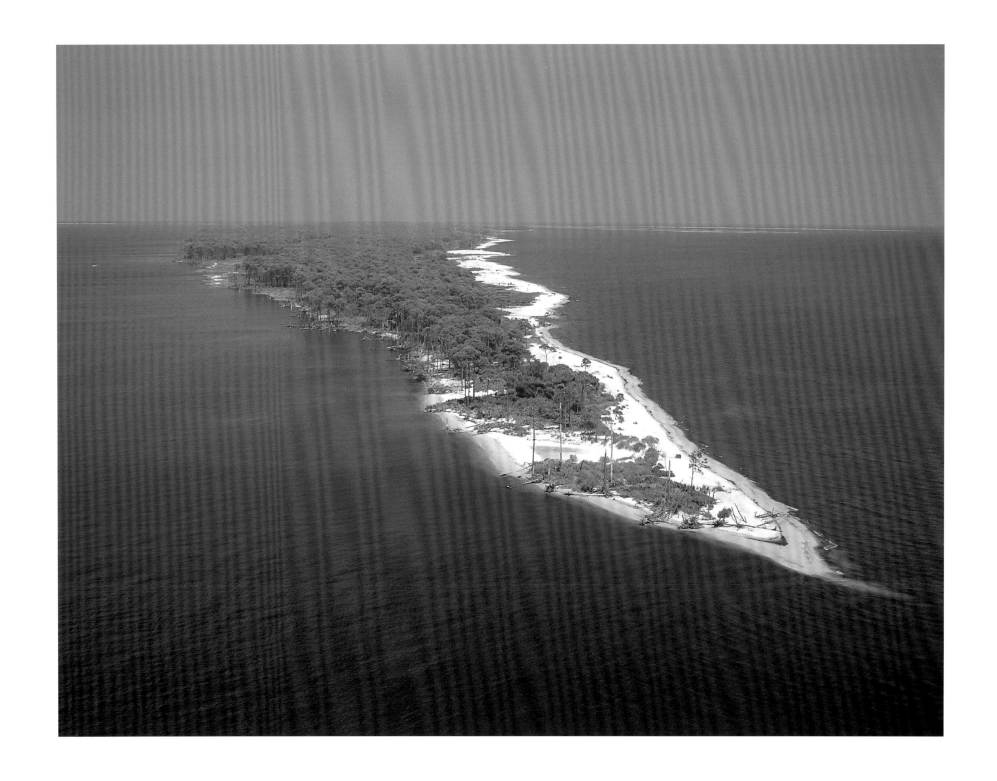

PLATE 58: *West end, Cat Island*

PLATE 59: *Ft. Massachusetts, Ship Island National Seashore*

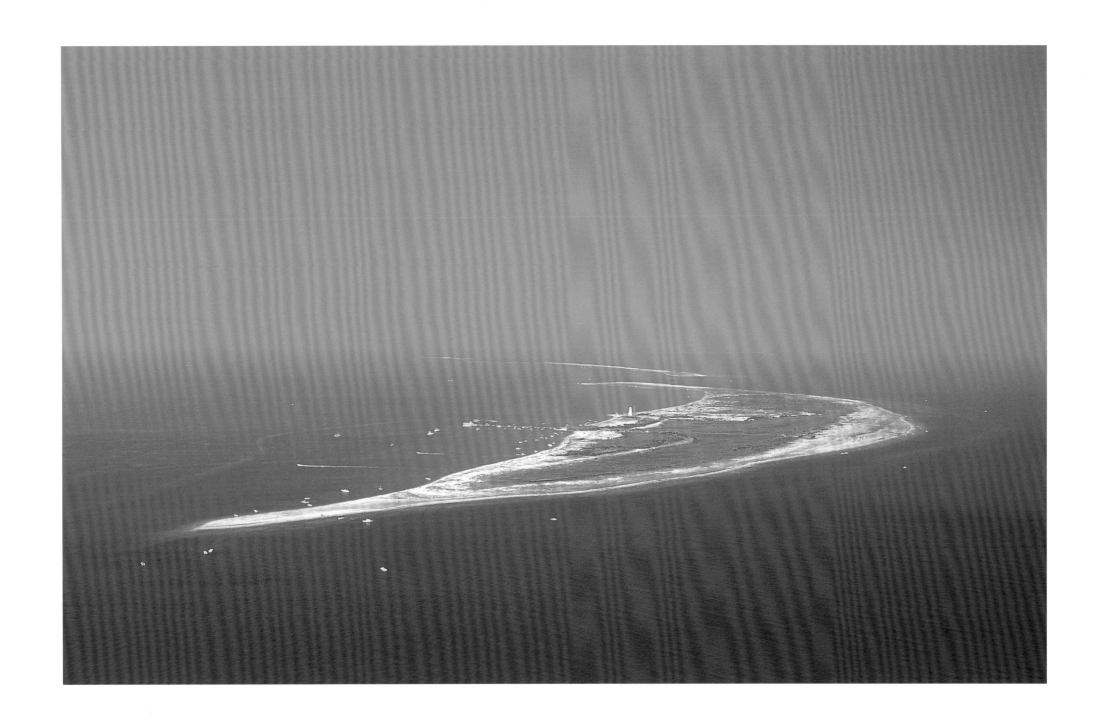

PLATE 60: *Ship Island National Seashore*

PLATE 61: *Sand dunes, Ship Island National Seashore*

81

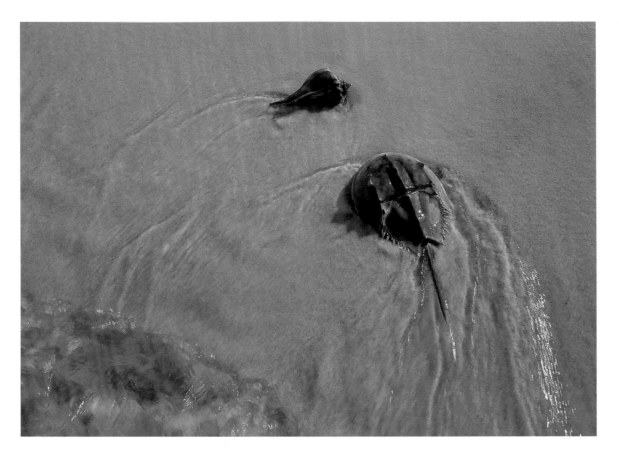
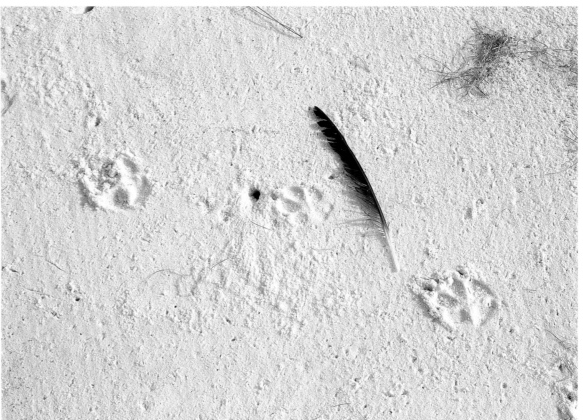

PLATE 62: *Conch and horseshoe crab, Horn Island*
PLATE 63: *Red Wolf tracks, Horn Island*

PLATE 64: *Sea Oats, Horn Island*

PLATE 65: *Henderson Point, Pass Christian*

PLATE 66: *Scenic Drive, Pass Christian*

87

PLATE 67: *University of Southern Mississippi, Long Beach*

PLATE 68: *La Maison Gautier, circa 1867, Gautier*

PLATE 69: *Long Beach Small Craft Harbor, Long Beach*

PLATE 70: *Eight Flags, East Beach Blvd., Gulfport*
PLATE 71: *The Sensation at the Port of Gulfport and the Gulfport Small Craft Harbor, Gulfport*

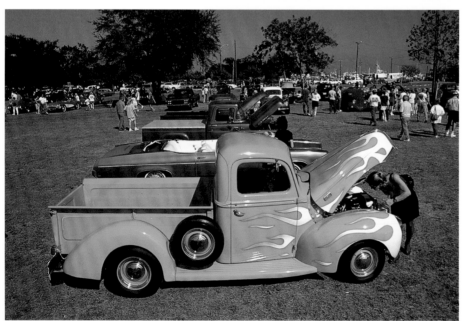

PLATE 72: *Cruisin' the Coast, 2000, Gulfport*
PLATE 73: *Cruisin' the Coast, 2000, Pass Christian*
PLATE 74: *Rice Pavilion, Cruisin' the Coast, 1999, Gulfport*

PLATE 75: *Rice Pavilion, Cruisin' the Coast, 1999, Gulfport*

95

PLATE 76: *Country Road, Stone County*

97

PLATE 77: *Shearwater Pottery, Ocean Springs*

99

PLATE 78: *Kudzu covering an abandoned house, Stone County*

PLATE 79: *Antique shop, Lucedale*

PLATE 80: *Making cane syrup, Stone County*

103

PLATE 81: *Goats and barn, Wool Market*

105

PLATE 82: *Wool Market*

107

PLATE 84: *Original Barq's Root Beer Factory, Biloxi*

111

PLATE 85: *Beauvoir, last home of Jefferson Davis, Biloxi*

113

PLATE 86: *Hall, Union Quarters, Pass Christian*

114

PLATE 87: *Union Quarters, Pass Christian*

PLATE 88: *Beach Blvd., Gulfport*

PLATE 89: *Church of the Redeemer, Biloxi*

118

PLATE 90: *Town Green at Christmas, Biloxi*

PLATE 91: *Scenic Drive, Pass Christian*

121

PLATE 92: *Tullis-Toledano Manor at Christmas, Biloxi*

122

PLATE 93: *Christmas on the Water boat parade winner,* Keesler, *1999, Biloxi*

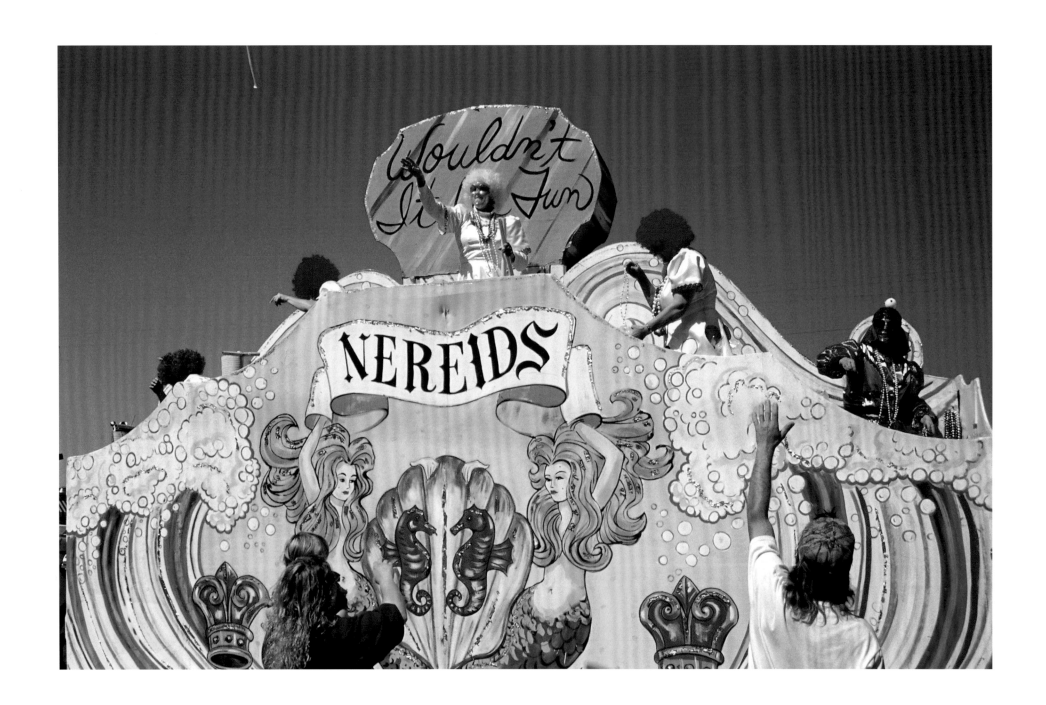

PLATE 94: *Nereids, Mardi Gras Parade, Waveland*

124

PLATE 95 AND 96: *Mardi Gras float, Pass Christian*

125

PLATE 97: *Round Island Lighthouse, Jackson County*

127

PLATE 98: *Original President Casino, Biloxi*

129

PLATE 99: *Copa Casino, Gulfport*

PLATE 100: *Biloxi Shoreline*

PLATE 101: *Casino Row, Biloxi*

PLATE 103: *Beau Rivage Marina, Biloxi*

138

PLATE 104: *Beau Rivage and the* Starship, *Biloxi*

PLATE 105: *The Point, Biloxi*

140

PLATE 106: *Casino Magic, Bay St. Louis*

PLATE 109: *South Beach Blvd, Bay St. Louis*

145

Acknowledgments

I have been putting off writing this part of the book until the last moment. There are so many people I want to thank, not only for helping with this book, but in life in general, that I am afraid of forgetting someone. If I do, please forgive me! To those areas of the Coast where I do not have many photographs, my apologies. I need more time and money.

First and foremost, I want to thank my wife Tina, who has worked extremely hard for twenty years in the "8 a.m.–7 p.m. grind," which has afforded me the ability to do the work I love to do. Also to my kids, who have made sacrifices. I can't forget to thank Tina's mother Marjorie Morrealle for her help with the kids. I love you all!

A special thanks to my business partners and brothers, Ray and Audie "Rock" Murphy, who are currently serving as UN Police in Kosovo. Also thanks to my brother Tim Murphy and his partner Dorothy Susan Boegner, who were there to help when called upon.

My mother Helen Murphy Decell and stepfather Louis Decell have done more than I'll ever be able to repay. Thank you very much!

Without Ed Gemmill, who, when I proposed this project, barely had to think about it before he jumped on board, there would not be a book project.

David Washer of Coast Community Bank made the financing of this book a very quick and pleasurable experience. Thank you very much!

Mike Olivier, Executive Director of the Harrison County Development Commission, was the first to show his support by committing to purchase the book when it was still just an idea. He brought Gary LaGrange, Executive Director at the Port of Gulfport, on board, which led to commitments from Asher Travis and Tina Ross-Seamans of Gulfshores, Inc., as well as Ann Hoff of the Beau Rivage and Mayor A. J. Holloway of Biloxi. It was their confidence in my photography that provided the investor confidence that we needed to move forward. Thank you all very much!

A special thanks to Charles "Chuck" and Nancy Ramsey of Bay Tec in Bay St. Louis, who supported my photography ten years ago by purchasing my work and participating in my New Orleans poster project.

Also, thanks to Joe and Mary Sheeran and pilot Dan Walker of Vortex Helicopters, whom I use exclusively for all my aerial work.

A very special thank you goes to Chris Trapani for saving me countless hours and gallons of gas by taking my film to the lab on his way to work in New Orleans.

The only thing I can say about designer John Langston is, WOW! Thanks man! I brought John a dummy book (I destroyed my copy of *Faulkner's Mississippi* making it) and a "pile" of about seven hundred photographs, and in very short order he gave me a real book. Great job!

Also on the team were Ginger Tucker and Bill Pitts (Bill drew the map in the front of this book).

Thanks to Jim Miller who was responsible for many location assignments featured in this book.

Finally, thanks to Bruce Bourgeois for showing me his favorite locations to shoot.

Thank you for purchasing this book, which really is the ultimate compliment. I hope you enjoy it.

Photographer's Note

These notes are provided to educate and entertain. However, I freely admit that I am the world's worst record keeper. Some of these notes are based on my memory, which can be faulty. Many of these scenes have been altered by storms and/or development; most of the skiffs are gone. Things are changing.

My cameras are: 35mm Format—Nikon n90s and FMII; Medium Format—Mamiya 645 Pro; 4x5—Calumet Cambo Woodfield and Calumet Cambo Wide.

Most of the photographs in this book were shot on Kodak transparency film, with one or two exceptions—the aerial of Imperial Palace, which was shot on negative film, for example. Usually, my film of choice is Ektachrome 64T (85B filter), 100Plus, 100SW, 100VS, or 100S (usually with a polarizing filter). The film size formats vary from 35mm to 4x5, with 4x5 being my preferred format. (For you non-photographers, 4x5 refers to the size of the film which is 4 inches by 5 inches. Medium format, commonly referred to as 120mm, which is the length of the roll, averages approximately 2 inches by 3 inches, and 35mm film is approximately 1 inch by 3/4 inch. Technically speaking, the larger the film format, the higher the photographic quality.) At a minimum, I note the film format and type, then any pertinent information. Most images shot on 64T had an 85b correction filter unless otherwise noted. Also, all aerial photos were shot from a helicopter.

I have never been, or will I ever be, a "gadgeteer." Very high quality photography can be created using inexpensive equipment. Knowing how the photographic process works and which films to use for any given subject is essential—but the key is passion.

Finally, a special thanks to Missy Maciuck for convincing me to add the photographer's notes.

TECHNICAL INFORMATION

Page

i. Med. Format, 100SW. Luck is a big part of capturing the moment. Notice the sailboat in the moonlight.

ii. 4x5, 100Plus.

iii. 4x5, 100Plus.

iv. 4x5, 64T. This was shot near the head of St. Charles St. in Bay St. Louis on a cold winter morning.

vi. 4x5, 64T.

x. 4x5, 64T. St. Stanislaus was founded in 1854 and is the largest Catholic Boys Boarding School in Mississippi.

xii. 4x5, 100Plus.

1. 4x5, 64T. This is a cold winter sunrise also. The cold air and low humidity helps create sharp, vivid color.

PLATES

1. 4x5, 64T. Another cold winter sunrise.

2. 4x5, 64T. If you want to shoot in this environment, be sure to have long sleeve everything, including a mosquito head net and copious amounts of bug spray.

3.&4. 4x5, 64T. Casino Magic is located just outside the frame on the right.

5. 4x5, 64T. The buildings on the horizon are Bordages Fish Camp.

6. 35mm.

7. 4x5, 64T. Bordages Fish Camp was founded in 1926 near the mouth of Bayou Caddy and moved to its current location in the 1930s. It was completely destroyed in the 1947 hurricane and again by Camille in 1969. It is currently operated by Tommy Bordage.

8. 35mm, 100Plus.

9. 35mm, 100Plus.

10. 35mm, Kodachrome 64.

11. 35mm, 100Plus. This shot was done on assignment. My apologies to the model, whom I don't remember.

12. 35mm, 100SW. When I was growing up around here, pelicans were a rare sight and the old timers used to talk about the old days when there was a "pelican on every post." These are brown pelicans and are now one of my favorite subjects.

13. 35mm, 100SW.

14. 35mm, 100Plus.

15. 35mm, 100SW.

16. 35mm, 100SW.

17. Med. Format, 100SW.

18. 4x5, 64T.

19. 4x5, 100Plus. This is one of those scenes that has changed. The pier is currently in disrepair.

20. Med. Format, 100SW.

21. 4x5, 64T. This pier is gone. The Bay / Waveland Yacht Club is just to the right.

22. 35mm, 100SW. This is my nephew Brandon Grogg and my niece Maddison Murphy.

23. Med. Format, 100SW. I am the official Cruisin' the Coast photographer. It is one of my favorite assignments. Thanks to Gene Oswalt, Ex. Director.

24. Med. Format, 100SW. I rode in the back of John Mahners's pickup to get this shot. We drove up and down Highway 90 until we (the film crew) were satisfied. Thanks to Bill and Norma Gates of Gulfport, in the lead car, for gathering the vehicles.

25. 35mm, 100SW

26. 35mm, Kodachrome 64. It was my idea to rescue this gator, which had come out of a drainage ditch during a heavy rain. We released him in a more remote area. That's my cousin Steve Carver (with hat) and our friend Al Stoufflet.

27. 35mm, Kodachrome 64.

28. 4x5, 100Plus. Uncle Al, as we affectionately called him, even though he wasn't, cut three generations of Murphy hair. He always had a story or a joke.

29. 35mm, 100Plus. Circa 1810. This is the oldest United Methodist Church on the Coast.

30. 4x5, 64T. For info call 228-467-1772 or Gulfsideassembly@earthlink.net

31. 35mm, Kodachrome 64.

32. 4x5, 64T. Circa 1870. I just discovered that my great grandfather Pete Carver's brother Andrew and his wife Emma

lived here in the 1930s. It is the home of Charles Cresson now.

33. 4x5, 64T. Circa 1818. Home of Chuck and Ellen Breath.

34. 4x5, 64T. This was the first seminary in America created to educate African Americans. Founded in 1926.

35. Med. Format, 100SW. The mural depicts a black Jesus rising from the dead.

36. 4x5, 64T.

37. 4x5, 64T, no filter.

38. 4x5, 64T. Although I did not know it when I made this photograph, this gravesite turned out to be the family of my uncle Vernon Murphy's wife, Vera Koch Murphy.

39. 4x5, 64T. Wheat community, Hwy. 43.

40. 4x5, 64T. Crosby Arboretum is open to the public. Call 601-799-2311.

41. 4x5, 100Plus. Prior to 1969 Tung trees were a major industry as a source of fine oils.

42. Med. Format, 100SW.

43. 35mm, 100SW.

44. Med. Format, 100SW.

45. Med. Format, 100SW.

46. Med. Format, 100SW.

47. 4x5, 64T. This is the Railroad Bar at Railroad and Waveland avenues.

48. 4x5, 64T.

49. 4x5, 100Plus.

50. 35mm, 100SW.

51. 35mm, 100SW.

52. 35mm, 100SW. Photographed on St. Stanislaus campus.

53. Med. Format, 100SW.

54. 4x5, 64T.

55. Med. Format, 100Plus. Thanks to Dr. John Green for allowing me to photograph on his property and supporting my work.

56. Med. Format, 100SW.

57. Med. Format, 100SW.

58. Med. Format, 100SW.

59. 35mm, 100SW. Built between 1859 and 1866. This is actually two photos that have been spliced together. The fort is

open to the public. Call 228-875-9057.

60. Med. Format, 100SW.

61. Med. Format, 100SW.

62. Med. Format, 100SW.

63. Med. Format, 100SW. Just before I made this photo, I was fortunate enough to see a Red Wolf coming up the beach behind me. As soon as he saw that I was watching him, he was gone.

64. Med. Format, 100SW. In the boat on the horizon is Truman Schultz, a life-long friend, who was my ride to the island. He alerted me to the wolf on the beach.

65. Med. Format, 100SW.

66. 4x5, 64T.

67. Med. Format, 100Plus.

68. 4x5, 64T.

69. Med. Format, 100SW.

70. 35mm, 100Plus. This was shot before the Confederate flag controversy. The flags have since been removed but the display is supposed to be restored in the near future.

71. Med. Format, 100SW.

72. Med. Format, 100SW.

73. Med. Format, 100SW.

74. Med. Format, 100SW.

75. Med. Format, 100SW.

76. 4x5, 64T.

77. 4x5, 64T.

78. 4x5, 64T.

79. 4x5, 100Plus. This is one of my favorite photographs. The gentleman had to have his "Michael Jackson" doll in the shot. Notice the placement of the doll's hand. They had a great sense of humor.

80. 4x5, 64T. The Derlyn Bond family makes syrup every Thanksgiving at 1158 Hwy 15N. About 20 miles north of Biloxi.

81. 4x5, 64T.

82. 4x5, 64T. Circa 1820. Known as The Old Stiglets Place.

83. 4x5, 64T. Circa 1848.

84. Med. Format, 100SW. Circa 1895.

85. 4x5, 64T. Circa 1851.

86. 4x5, 64T.

87. 4x5, 64T. During the Civil War and the Union occupation of the Coast, this home served as the headquarters of the Union Army on the Coast.

88. 4x5, 64T.

89. 4x5, 64T. This bell tower is all that remained of the church after Hurricane Camille.

90. Med. Format, 100SW.

91. 4x5, 64T. Home of the Charles and Nancy Ramsey family. Built in 1964.

92. 4x5, 64T. Circa 1856. Tullis-Toledano Manor is located at 360 East Beach Blvd. and is open to the public.

93. 4x5, 64T.

94. 35mm, 100SW.

95. 35mm, 100.

96. 35mm, 100.

97. 35mm, 100SW. Circa 1833. In 1998, the Round Island Lighthouse Society was established. Shortly thereafter, Hurricane Georges caused major damage. It is currently being restored. Anyone wishing to join the effort to save this important landmark is urged to contact Betty Bensey at 228-938-6639.

98. Med. Format, 64T.

99. Med. Format, 100SW.

100. 35mm, 100SW. I was pleased that this photo held together so well for such an enlargement from 35mm. I attribute that to the 200LPI printing.

101. Med. Format, 100SW.

102. 4x5, 64T. This photograph was shot from the top of the Grand Hotel Biloxi.

103. Med. Format, Portra 400. This photo was scanned from a print.

104. Med. Format, 100SW.

105. Med. Format, Portra 400. This photo was scanned from a print.

106. 4x5, 64T.

107. 35mm, 100SW.

108. 35mm, 100Plus. Again, luck plays a major part in photography.

109. 4x5, 64T.